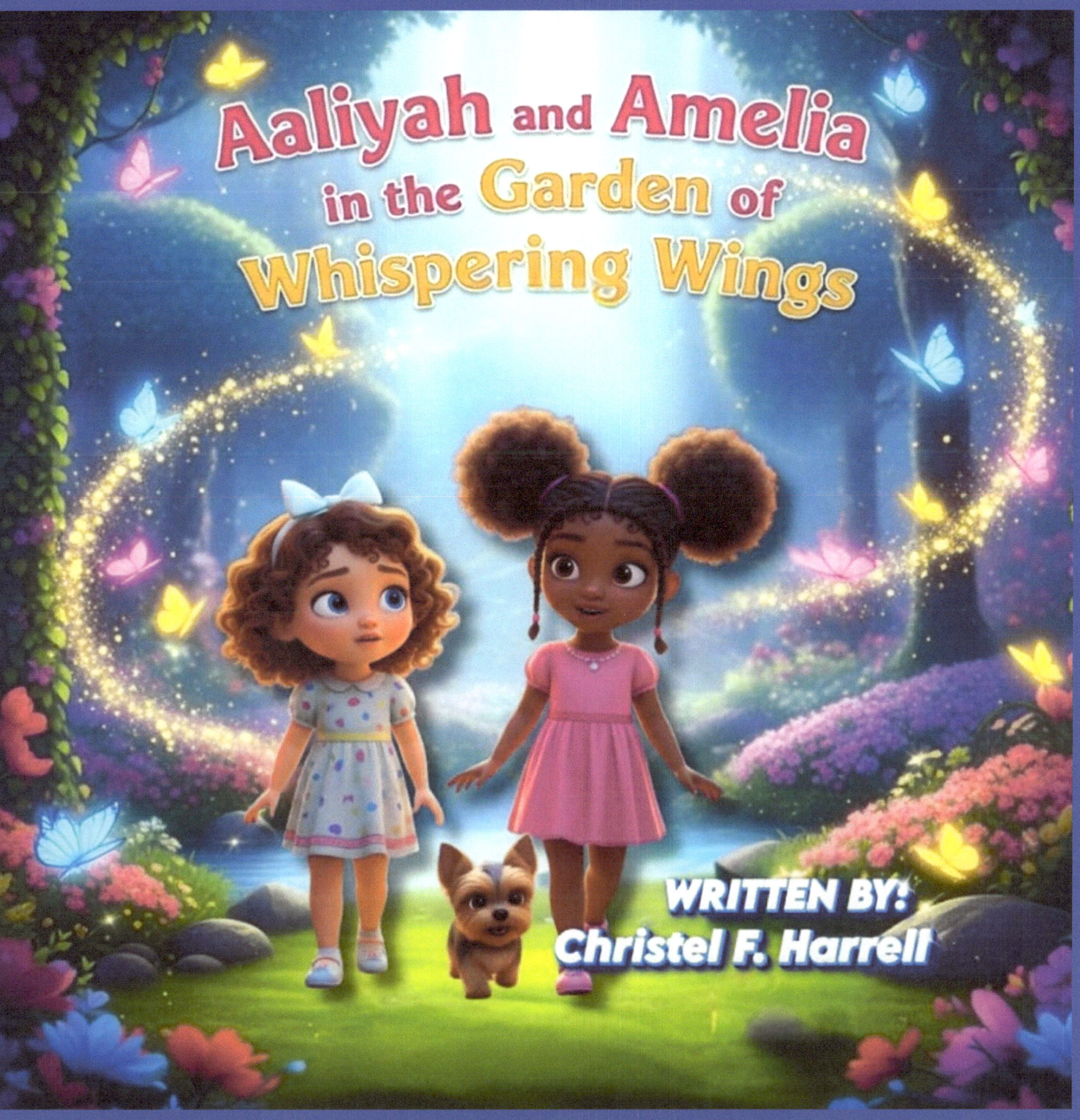
Aaliyah and Amelia
in the Garden of
Whispering Wings
WRITTEN BY:
Christel F. Harrell

Dedication

To my mother,
A three-time cancer survivor whose love of butterflies has become a family symbol of transformation, resilience, and hope.

To my granddaughter, Amelia, and my great-niece, Aaliyah—two amazing girls who inspired this story. Your gentle spirit and bold laughter show the world that every voice matters. The story features the family's yorkie, Zeekie, whose playful spirit reminds us of the importance of joy and companionship.

May this book encourage everyone that reads this book to embrace their uniqueness,
be confident in who they are and always remember the power of their voice.

About the Author

Christel Finley-Harrell is an author, entrepreneur, Certified Life Coach, and community leader with a passion for serving others. She is the founder of a nonprofit organization that supports single women, single women with children, and families through education and empowerment. While Christel writes to inspire readers of all ages, this heartwarming book is written especially for children and preteens—encouraging them to embrace their uniqueness, build confidence, and discover the power of their voice.

TABLE OF CONTENT

Aaliyah and Amelia in the Garden of Whispering Wings

Chapter One: The Butterfly with a Secret

There were once two young sisters in Willowbrook, Aaliyah and Amelia. Aaliyah loved to sing, dress up, and put on shows for her dolls. Amelia was quieter, content to have her hair brushed or to sit with their Yorkie, Zeekie. She liked to watch, to listen, and to notice things others missed. Still, she loves playing on the swingset too, especially when her sister is beside her. The sisters play together in the backyard on the swingset, Aaliyah soaring high while Amelia pushes gently with a thoughtful smile. Zeekie barks and runs circles around them.

A sudden shimmer floats through the air. At first, it looks like a beam of sunlight, but then it flutters its wings. It is a butterfly. Not just any butterfly. Its wings gleam like rainbows, changing colors from pink, gold, ocean blue, and emerald green. "Whoa!" Aaliyah gasps, reaching out. "Amelia, look!" Amelia narrows her eyes as she whispers. "It's beautiful."

The butterfly hovers closer. Its voice sounds like soft wind chimes. "My name is Zoe," it says. "And I've been looking for you." Both girls freeze. A butterfly that talks? "You can talk?!" Aaliyah squeals. "This is amazing!" as she giggles Amelia clutches her drawing pad and asks shyly. "Why?" Zoe lands on Aaliyah's hand. "I come from a hidden garden where butterflies shine brighter than stars. But our colors are fading. We are disappearing. I was sent to find children with strong voices. One brave. One wise. Together, you can save us."

Aaliyah grins so wide her cheeks turn red. "See, Amelia? We're chosen heroes!" Amelia frowns. "We're just kids. We can't stop the butterflies from fading." "Believing is the first step," Zoe says. "If you don't, our colors vanish forever." Aaliyah's eyes sparkle with excitement, but Amelia chews her lip. She's not sure she wants to go, but when her sister squeezes her hand, Amelia sighs. "Okay." Zoe flutters into the air, scattering golden dust that shapes itself into a glowing path. "Follow me." Zeekie bounces after the sisters as they step onto the path, waggling his tail. And the adventure begins.

Chapter Two: The Fading Garden

The glowing trail carries them beyond the backyard, through a swirl of light, until the air smells sweet like honey and flowers. They find themselves standing in a fairy garden. Huge blossoms glow in shades of pink and blue. A silver stream trickles through crystal rocks. Butterflies drift everywhere, but their wings look pale, gray, and almost invisible.

Aaliyah gasps. "They look sick." Amelia nods softly. "Like the color's been washed away." They are fading. A cluster of weak butterflies gathers around Zoe. One whispers, "Did you find them?" "Yes," Zoe says proudly. "These are the sisters. They can help us."

Amelia shakes her head. "We don't know what to do." How can we help save the butterflies? "You do," Zoe replies gently. "The colors return when children find their voices and the courage to be who they are. Each time you discover your strength, a new color will bloom again." The sisters exchange a look. Aaliyah is thrilled. Amelia is doubtful. But the first test comes quickly.

Chapter Three: The First Voice

A towering branch blocks their way, its vines so thick that no path can be seen. From deep within, a faint red glow flickers, like a lantern waiting to be found. "The way is hidden," Zoe says softly. "Only the right call can awaken it." Aaliyah steps forward with her usual eagerness. "I'll try!" She cups her hands and shouts, "Open up!" The branch rustles, but nothing moves.

Amelia bites her lip, then tugs Aaliyah's sleeve. "Maybe it's not about shouting louder... maybe it's about saying what we really feel." Aaliyah pauses, thinking. She takes Amelia's hand. Together, the sisters close their eyes and speak as one: "We're here to help. Please let us through." The branch trembles. Slowly, the vines untangle and curl back, opening into a tunnel glowing with red light.

At that very moment, a butterfly flutters nearby, its wings shimmering into a brilliant ruby red. "You did it together!" Zoe cheers. "That is the First Voice, the voice of courage." Aaliyah beams. Amelia squeezes her sister's hand, her smile small but certain.

Chapter four: The Second Voice

The path leads to a still pond. The water reflects the sky, but the reflection of the sisters is blurry. Suddenly, the water is calm and quiet. "This test," Zoe explains, "is about truth." Amelia feels her chest tighten. She doesn't like speaking up. But something inside whispers that this is her turn to be heard. She kneels by the pond. "I'm Amelia," she says softly. "I'm scared a lot. I don't like to talk. But... I want to help."

Her reflection is clear. A butterfly near the pond glows into a deep, calm blue. Aaliyah squeezes her sister's hand. "That was amazing, Amelia." For the first time, Amelia smiles without being afraid.

Chapter Five – The Garden of Voices

The sisters journey deeper. Each challenge asks them to use a different part of themselves, laughter to cheer a wilting flower, teamwork to guide Zeekie across a shaky bridge, honesty, and when they quarrel and must make up. They also learn to share. Every time they succeed, another butterfly regains its color: orange for joy, yellow for kindness, green for hope, and purple for wisdom.

The garden brightens. Flowers sparkle. Streams sing. But one butterfly remains pale, its wings almost gone. Zoe's glow dims. "Only one color is missing. The hardest one."

Chapter Six – The Final Color

At the heart of the garden stands a stone archway. Behind it, a swirling darkness spreads. The last butterfly hovers weakly nearby. "This test," Zoe says, "is about love. The strongest voice of all." Suddenly, the ground shakes. The archway crackles with dark vines. Zeekie barks as a shadowy wind pulls him toward the arch. "Zeekie!" Aaliyah cries, rushing forward.

Amelia freezes, terrified. The vines twist together as they move closer. Aaliyah pulls and shouts, but Zeekie slips. "Help me, Amelia!" she pleads. Amelia's whole body trembles. She wants to run. But then she looks at her sister, fighting bravely, and at Zeekie's scared eyes. Something inside her breaks open.

"I love you!" she screams. "I won't let anything take you away!" With those words, light bursts from her chest. The vines shatter. Zeekie tumbles into their arms, safe. The last butterfly's wings blaze into brilliant gold. The garden explodes in color. Red, blue, orange, yellow, green, purple, and gold, all glowing brighter than rainbows.

Chapter Seven: The Lesson of the Garden

The butterflies swirl around the sisters, wings shimmering. The once-faded colony now glows like living jewels. "You did it," Zoe says, landing on Amelia's shoulder. "You found your voices. Courage, truth, joy, kindness, hope, wisdom, and love. Together, you brought back the colors." Aaliyah grins proudly. "We're heroes after all! We saved the butterflies together."

Amelia hugs Zeekie close. "We're just... us. But that was enough. All we needed was each other." The butterflies lift into the sky, filling the garden with light. One by one, the colors settle back into the flowers, streams, and trees.

Zoe flutters before them. "The garden will always remember you. And whenever you speak with courage and kindness in your world, our colors will never fade again." The sisters blink and suddenly, they are back in their backyard. The sun shines as if nothing happened. Except… a single glowing butterfly lands on Amelia's drawing pad as she sits on the swingset. It is Zoe.

"Remember," she whispers. "Your voices are stronger than you think." Then she lifts off, leaving a trail of golden sparkles that slowly fade into the sky. Aaliyah laughs, spinning in the grass. "Best. Day. Ever! Our voice matters!" Amelia smiles softly. For once, she agrees. She simply opens her drawing pad and begins to draw two sisters, a dog, and a butterfly with wings of every color.

And deep in Willowbrook, the Color Garden shines again. There is magic in your voice.

Design Your Own Butterfly

Every butterfly is unique, just like you!
Use your favorite colors and designs
to create your own special butterfly.

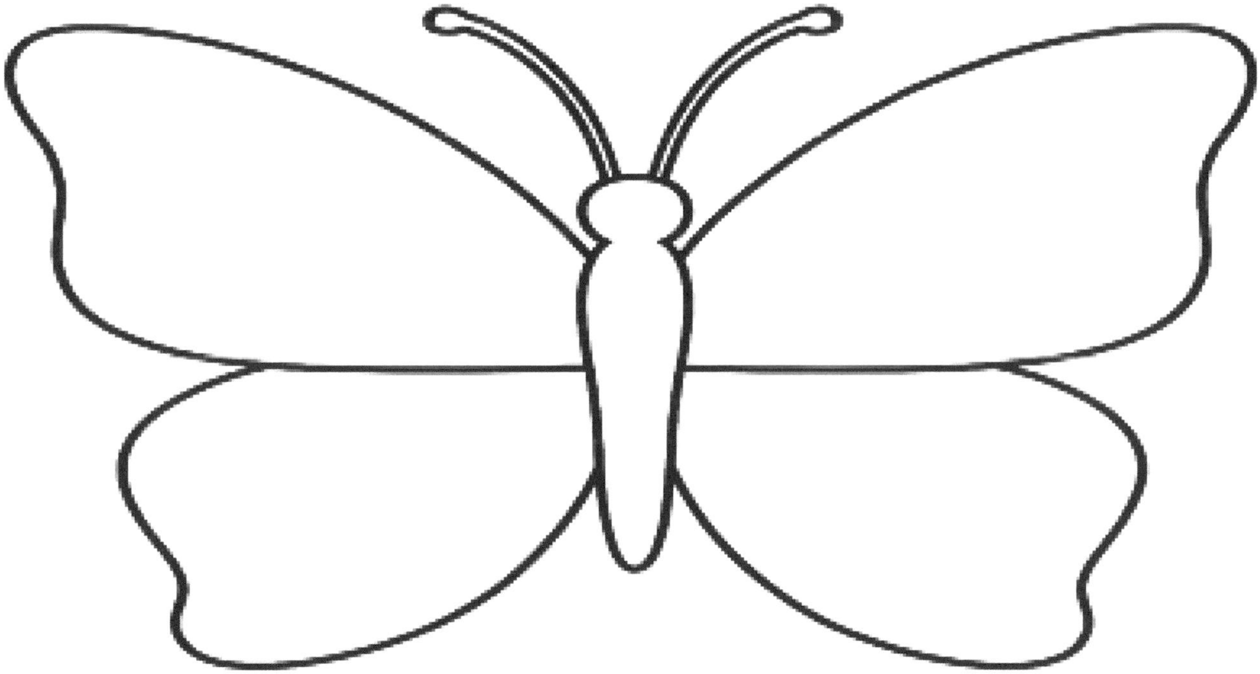

HELP THE BUTTERFLY FIND ITS WAY TO THE FLOWER GARDEN!

Color Your Feelings

Butterflies change colors, and so do our feelings! Color each butterfly to show how you feel today:

Happy Sad Excited Brave

50

51

ABOUT THE BOOK

To every little girl who has ever felt too small, too shy, or too scared, this story is for you. May you always find your wings, trust your voice, and know that you are braver than you believe. And to the butterflies who guide us with whispers of courage, thank you for reminding us that we can shine in our own beautiful way.

www.ingramcontent.com/pod-product-compliance
Ingram Content Group UK Ltd.
Pitfield, Milton Keynes, MK11 3LW, UK
UKHW061031310726
14089UKWH00009B/196